T0168262

TAGINES

TAGINES

Explore the traditional tastes of North Africa,
with 30 authentic recipes

Ghillie Başan

Photography by Martin Brigdale

This edition is published by Aquamarine,
an imprint of Anness Publishing Ltd,
108 Great Russell Street, London WC1B 3NA;
info@anness.com

www.aquamarinebooks.com;
www.annesspublishing.com; twitter: @Anness_Books

If you like the images in this book and would
like to investigate using them for publishing,
promotions or advertising, please visit our website
www.practicalpictures.com for more information.

Publisher: Joanna Lorenz
Editor: Kate Eddison
Photographer: Martin Brigdale
Food stylists: Annie Rigg, Lucy McKelvie and Linda Tubby
Prop stylists: Martin Brigdale and Helen Trent
Designer: Lisa Tai
Indexer: William Jack
Production controller: Pirong Wang

Some recipes in this book previously appeared in *Modern Moroccan*.

NOTES

- Bracketed terms are intended for American readers.
- For all recipes, quantities are given in both metric and imperial measures and, where appropriate, in standard cups and spoons. Follow one set of measures, but not a mixture, because they are not interchangeable.
- Standard spoon and cup measures are level. 1 tsp = 5ml, 1 tbsp = 15ml, 1 cup = 250ml/8fl oz.
- Australian standard tablespoons are 20ml. Australian readers should use 3 tsp in place of 1 tbsp for measuring small quantities.
- American pints are 16fl oz/2 cups. American readers should use 20fl oz/2.5 cups in place of 1 pint when measuring liquids.
- Electric oven temperatures in this book are for conventional ovens. When using a fan oven, the temperature will probably need to be reduced by about 10–20°C/20–40°F. Since ovens vary, you should check with your manufacturer's instruction book for guidance.
- The nutritional analysis given for each recipe is calculated per portion (i.e. serving or item), unless otherwise stated. If the recipe gives a range, such as Serves 4–6, then the nutritional analysis will be for the smaller portion size, i.e. 6 servings. The analysis does not include optional ingredients, such as salt added to taste.
- Medium (US large) eggs are used unless otherwise stated.

Front cover shows *Chicken K'dra with Turnip and Ras El Hanout* – for recipe, see page 36.

PUBLISHER'S NOTE

Although the advice and information in this book are believed to be accurate and true at the time of going to press, neither the authors nor the publisher can accept any legal responsibility or liability for any errors or omissions that may have been made nor for any inaccuracies nor for any loss, harm or injury that comes about from following instructions or advice in this book.

CREDITS

The publisher would like to thank the following for permission to reproduce their images (t = top, b = bottom, l = left, r = right): 6b, 7t and 30b Martin Brigdale; 16b, 40l, 50l, 54b, 60r, 70b, 73b and 74l iStockphoto.

CONTENTS

Ancient cuisine

Perched at the north-west corner of the African continent, Morocco acts as a culinary gateway to the influences of central and northern Africa, to the ancient food traditions of the Arab world to the east, and to the Andalucian flavours of southern Spain across the water. Tagines embody this diverse collection of tastes and textures, and have become the symbol of Moroccan cuisine around the world.

Morocco is a land where the medieval and the modern are atmospherically intertwined, through geography, architecture and culture. From the impressive Atlas mountains to the majestic cities of ancient dynasties, and from the southern deserts to the sun-drenched coastline, Morocco's rich culinary culture has developed to reflect its varied landscape.

HISTORY AND CULTURE

The Arabs, who invaded the region between the seventh and fourteenth centuries, brought spices, nuts and fruits, some of which were incorporated into the Persian-inspired meat tagines. They also brought Islam and its dietary restrictions, which include specific rules for the slaughtering of an animal and the prohibition of consuming pork. The Moors, who were expelled from Spain, introduced olives, olive oil, tomatoes and paprika, and the Jewish refugees fleeing the Spanish Inquisition brought with them valuable preserving techniques, epitomized in the ubiquitous preserved lemons. The Ottoman Turks also left their mark with complex pastry-making and kebabs, and the Spanish and French, who colonized sections of Morocco, had a lasting influence on the cooking styles, with soups and sophisticated fish dishes, café culture, wine-making, and language. Even today, many of the dishes cooked in Morocco are known by their French names.

THE BERBERS

At the heart of the Moroccan culinary culture is the indigenous Berber population, with their simple, traditional dishes and their gifts of tagines and couscous. The Berbers have lived in North Africa, between Egypt and the western coast of Morocco, as far back as the archeological records go, and aspects of their cultural life are depicted on rocks across the Sahara Desert. Originally farmers, living alongside the nomadic Taureg and Bedouin of the desert, the Berbers made an impact on the food of the region long before the invasion of the Arabs. Although the Berbers had to convert from Christianity to Islam and adopt new religious and culinary customs, they attempt to keep their Berber heritage alive. Many rural Berber communities speak their own languages and dialects, and are fiercely proud of their ancestry and culinary traditions, which range from the simple roasting of meats over an open fire to the creation of the elaborate and aromatic tagines of the old imperial cities of the Berber dynasties – Marrakesh, Fes, Meknes and Rabat. These wonderful dishes, redolent of warming spices and seasonings, echo the lavish cuisines of medieval Baghdad and Moorish Spain.

Left: *The shape and size of a tagine often represent the Berber tribe or city from where it originates.*

CULINARY CULTURE

Food and family are the heartbeat of Moroccan culture. Daily life is centred around eating, with visits to the markets, tea in the cafés and endless street snacks. Most meals begin with a selection of little dishes to whet the appetite, which can range from marinated olives to puréed vegetable dips, savoury pastries, and tangy salads. A bowl of soup or a tagine might follow, served with a mound of couscous or fresh bread. Alternatively, the couscous may be served as a course on its own, as a celebratory dish or a palate cleanser. Grilled (broiled) or roasted meat, chicken or fish might follow, and fresh fruit usually completes the meal. On special occasions, the meal will end with a dessert, but most sweet dishes are enjoyed on their own as snacks, or they are offered as a gesture of hospitality. After the meal, hot mint tea is served to aid digestion.

Below: *Mint tea is served at the end of every meal in Morocco, and is a sign of hospitality.*

Above: *Aromatic and warming spices are used to create complex flavours in tagines.*

WHAT IS A TAGINE?

A tagine is a slow-cooked stew, deeply aromatic and full of flavour. The word 'tagine' is both the name of the cooked dish and the cooking vessel. Placed over a charcoal stove, which disperses the heat all around the base, a tagine enables the ingredients to cook gently in the steam, which builds up inside the lid, so that they remain beautifully tender and moist. At home, you can cook a tagine in the oven or on the stove top. Traditionally, a tagine will be served from the cooking vessel, with bread to mop up all the juices, but, in some regions, the contents of the tagine will be transferred to an ornate one, decorated with blue, turquoise, green, yellow and red patterns.

Many of the traditional tagines are distinguished by their cooking fats and spices: some are cooked in olive or argan oil, others are flavoured with smen or ghee; some are sweetened with honey and the floral notes of saffron and orange blossom water; some are spiced with chillies, ras el hanout and harissa; while others are prepared with tangy fruit, such as preserved lemons.

Cooking methods, such as browning and sautéing, and the quantity of liquid used, varies from the countryside to the cities. But for large numbers of people, such as at religious feasts and family celebrations, the traditional tagine is not big enough, so large tin-lined copper pots called k'dras are used instead. Most k'dra dishes are cooked in smen or ghee.

BUYING A TAGINE

Tagines come in various shapes and sizes. To be used for cooking, they must be glazed and soaked in water for 24 hours. Some also benefit from being seasoned (filled with a mixture of oil and water, or milk, then gently heated through to remove the earthenware taste and to prepare it for prolonged cooking over heat). Today, many tagines are sold with a diffuser for use on conventional stoves and gas hobs, but they can still develop tiny cracks. For hassle-free tagine cooking, invest in one with an earthenware conical lid but a cast-iron base.

Couscous

A staple throughout the whole of the North African region, couscous is Morocco's national dish. To the majority of Moroccans, a meal without couscous is unthinkable. It is traditionally served as a separate course, but it can also be served as an accompaniment to tagines, or grilled and roasted meats. Rubbed with oil, mixed with chopped herbs or sprinkled with spices, couscous is prepared with joy.

The word 'couscous' refers to the dried granules, as well as to the cooked dish. It is traditionally prepared in a 'couscoussier' – a two-tiered pot with a stewing section at the base for the meat, beans or vegetables, and a steaming pot on top for the couscous. Although referred to as a 'grain' it is not technically one; instead it could be described as Moroccan 'pasta' since it is made with various flours, which are mixed with water and hand-rolled.

TYPES OF COUSCOUS

There are many different types of couscous in Morocco, some made with wheat flour, others with barley, maize, or millet. In the rural villages, women take sacks of wheat to the local mill where it is ground into semolina. From this, they prepare couscous: they sprinkle water on to the semolina flour and rake it with their fingers to form small balls. These balls are passed through sieves (strainers) to make tiny granules. These are then spread out to dry.

In modern households in the cities, many cooks prefer to avoid this labour-intensive process and buy sacks of prepared couscous, which needs to be steamed several times before eating, or the pre-cooked granules which only require soaking in water to swell before use. (The recipes in this book employ the pre-cooked version, which is the standard variety available in most supermarkets outside Morocco).

Preparing couscous

This basic recipe for preparing couscous will produce fluffy and buttery results every time. Start preparations when your tagine has 30 minutes left to cook.

Serves 4

2.5ml/½ tsp salt
400ml/14fl oz/1⅔ cups warm water
350g/12oz/2 cups medium couscous
30ml/2 tbsp sunflower oil
knob (pat) of butter

1 Stir the salt into the water. Place the couscous in a bowl and cover with the water, stirring. Set aside for 10 minutes. Meanwhile, preheat the oven to 180°C/350°F/Gas 4. Using your fingers, rub the sunflower oil into the couscous.

2 Transfer the couscous to an ovenproof dish. Cut the knob of butter into tiny pieces, and arrange the butter on top of the couscous. Cover with foil, and heat in the oven for 20 minutes. Fluff up the couscous with a fork, and serve.

COUSCOUS TRADITIONS

For dietary, religious, and symbolic reasons, couscous is of fundamental value to Moroccan culinary culture. There are rituals for its preparation and many Moroccans believe that couscous brings God's blessing upon those who consume it. It is prepared in every Muslim household on holy days and on Fridays, the Islamic day of rest, when it is traditionally distributed to the poor as well. There is a Moroccan saying that 'each granule of couscous represents a good deed', which inevitably means that vast quantities of couscous are consumed every day.

It is an impressive sight when couscous is piled up in a cone-shaped mound for banquets and celebratory meals. Couscous is usually served as a communal dish, so the piles can be extraordinarily high. The traditional manner of eating couscous requires a little practice: once the mound has been set on the ground, or on the low table, the diners ram their right hands, palm upwards, into the grains to extract a handful, then expertly roll the grains between the thumb and the first two fingers to form small tight balls, which often contain small pieces of meat or vegetables as well, and then they flip these into their mouths with the greatest of ease. This tradition is the same for young and old, rich and poor, which means that the act of serving and eating couscous unites people all over Morocco. It is this strong culinary heritage that has made couscous the cornerstone of Moroccan and North African food culture.

Left: *Couscous is available in supermarkets around the world – it just needs to be soaked before use.*

Below: *For maximum flavour, oil is rubbed into soaked couscous to coat the grains, and chopped herbs are sometimes added too.*

Spices and flavourings

At the heart of tagine cooking are the spice mixes and flavourings that have been used for centuries. It is worth preparing some of the following basic recipes, since traditional ingredients such as preserved lemons, harissa paste, and chermoula marinade are essential if you wish to create authentic dishes. Most of these flavourings can now be purchased in supermarkets, but they are simple to make at home.

CHERMOULA

This traditional Moroccan marinade lends a hot and zesty flavour to grilled fish and vegetable dishes, and to some tagines. For speed, use a food processor or blender.

Makes enough for 1 recipe

2–3 garlic cloves, chopped
1–2 red chillies, deseeded and chopped
5–10ml/1–2 tsp cumin seeds
5ml/1 tsp coarse sea salt
a fingerful of saffron strands, soaked in 15ml/1 tbsp water
juice of 1 lemon
60ml/4 tbsp olive oil
a small bunch of fresh coriander (cilantro), finely chopped

1 Using a mortar and pestle, pound the garlic and chilli with the cumin seeds and salt to form a paste.
2 Beat in the saffron with the soaking water, lemon juice and the oil, and stir in the fresh coriander.
3 Transfer the mixture to a sterilized jar and store in the refrigerator for 1–2 weeks.

PRESERVED LEMONS

These are small, native, thin-skinned lemons, which are preserved in salt and lemon juice. The rind is chopped, then used for cooking and garnishing to impart a salty-citrus flavour.

Makes 10

10 unwaxed, organic lemons
150ml/10 tbsp sea salt
2 lemons, for squeezing

1 Wash and dry the lemons. Cut a thin slice from the top and bottom of each lemon. Set each lemon on one end and make two vertical cuts three quarters of the way through the fruit, so that the quarters are still attached at the base.
2 Stuff them with plenty of salt and pack them into a jar so that they are squashed together. Leave them for 3–4 days to allow the skins to soften.
3 Press them down again and pour in enough fresh lemon juice to cover them completely. Store the lemons for at least 1 month before using. Simply rinse off the salt and use them according to the recipe.

SMEN (AGED BUTTER)

An acquired taste, smen is pungent, as it is often flavoured with herbs and spices, and is left to mature in earthenware pots for months. It is a traditional speciality of the Berbers.

Makes 500g/1lb 2oz

500g/1lb 2oz unsalted butter, at room temperature
150ml/5fl oz water
15ml/1 tbsp sea salt
15ml/1 tbsp dried oregano

1 Soften the butter in a bowl. Boil the water with the salt and oregano to reduce it a little, then strain it directly on to the butter.
2 Stir the butter with a wooden spoon to make sure it is well blended and leave to cool.
3 Knead the butter with your hands to bind it, squeezing out the excess water. Drain well and spoon the butter into a hot, sterilized jar. Seal the jar and store it in a cool, dry place for at least 6 weeks. Once opened, store in the refrigerator and use within 1 week.

HARISSA

Prepared by pounding spices and fresh coriander (cilantro) with dried red chillies that have been soaked, or fresh chillies that have been roasted, harissa is a fiery paste. It is served as a condiment for meat, fish and vegetable dishes; it is added to marinades and sauces; and it is blended with yogurt or olive oil to make a dip. Jars of harissa are available in supermarkets.

Makes enough for a dip, or enough for several recipes

8 large dried red chillies, sliced open and deseeded
2 garlic cloves, crushed
2.5ml/½ tsp sea salt
2.5ml/½ tsp ground coriander
5ml/1 tsp ground cumin
45–60ml/3–4 tbsp olive oil
a small bunch of fresh coriander (cilantro), finely chopped

1 Soak the chillies in warm water for about 40 minutes, until soft. Drain and squeeze out the excess water.
2 Using a mortar and pestle, pound the chillies with the garlic and salt to form a paste. Beat in the ground coriander and cumin with enough of the oil to form a thick paste. Stir in the fresh coriander.
3 Spoon the mixture into a sterilized jar. Cover the harissa with a thin layer of olive oil, seal the jar, and keep it in the refrigerator for up to a month.

RAS EL HANOUT

This famous spice mix literally translates as 'the head of the shop'. It is a legendary mixture of at least thirty different spices, and every Moroccan spice merchant has his own recipe. It is impossible to recreate the complexity of genuine ras el hanout at home, but the following recipe conjures up a taste of the real thing.

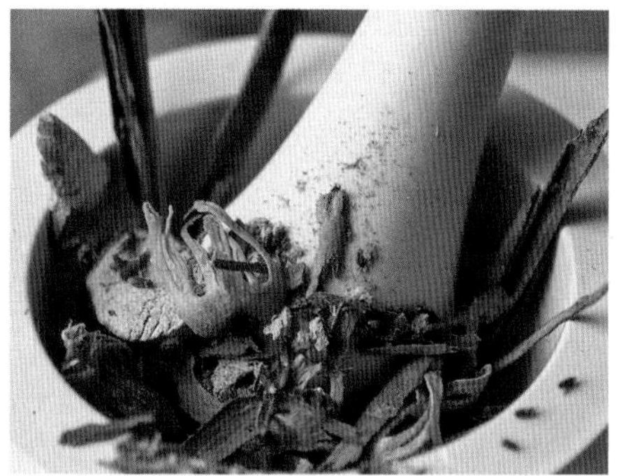

Makes enough to marinate several recipes

5ml/1 tsp black peppercorns
5ml/1 tsp cloves
5ml/1 tsp aniseeds
5ml/1 tsp nigella seeds
5ml/1 tsp allspice berries
5ml/1 tsp cardamom seeds
10ml/2 tsp ground ginger
10ml/2 tsp ground turmeric
10ml/2 tsp coriander seeds
2 pieces of mace
2 pieces cinnamon bark
10ml/2 tsp dried mint
1 dried red chilli
5ml/1 tsp dried lavender
6 dried rosebuds, broken up

1 Using a mortar and pestle, grind all the ingredients except the lavender and rose petals together to a coarse powder.
2 Add the lavender and rose petals, and transfer to a sealed container. Store for 6 months, away from direct sunlight.

MINT TEA

This is Morocco's national drink, offered throughout the day and served at the end of a meal as a digestive. It is prepared by brewing green tea with a huge bunch of fresh mint leaves, which are crammed into the teapot. Sometimes, the mint is combined with lemon verbena, geranium, or lemon balm leaves, and it is usually sweetened with large lumps of sugar.

Makes a pot for 4–6

10ml/2 tsp Chinese Gunpowder green tea
5ml/1 tsp sugar, plus extra to taste
a big bunch of fresh mint leaves, on their stalks

1 Put the green tea into a teapot with the sugar and a little boiling water. Put the lid on, and steep for 2–3 minutes.
2 Add the mint leaves to the pot, cramming in as many sprigs of mint as you can. Add more sugar to taste, and fill the teapot with boiling water. Put the lid back on, cover with a tea-cozy, or keep warm, and leave to steep for 5–10 minutes.
3 Pour a little of the tea into glasses or cups to warm them up, then pour the tea back into the pot so that it is well mixed.
4 Hold the teapot at an angle quite high above the glasses, or cups, and pour the tea, lowering and raising the pot so that a thin layer of froth forms on the tea.

Fish and shellfish

The tagines in this chapter celebrate the diverse flavours of the various fish and shellfish that are in constant supply from the Strait of Gibraltar and the Atlantic Ocean. Fish is commonly marinated in the aromatic spice paste chermoula, where the distinctive spice mix works beautifully with the delicate flesh. Prawns (shrimp), mussels and scallops are given special k'dra treatment in an extravagant dish fit for a feast.

Moroccan fish tagine

For me, this spicy, aromatic dish proves just how exciting an ingredient fish can be. Serve it with couscous, which you can steam in the traditional way in a colander on top of the tagine.

SERVES 8

1.3kg/3lb firm white fish fillets, such as monkfish or cod, skinned
90ml/6 tbsp harissa (*see* recipe page 11 or use store-bought)
60ml/4 tbsp olive oil
1 large aubergine (eggplant), cut into 1cm/½in cubes
2 courgettes (zucchini), cut into 1cm/½in cubes
4 onions, chopped
400g/14oz can chopped tomatoes
400ml/14fl oz/1⅔ cups passata (bottled strained tomatoes)
200ml/7fl oz/scant 1 cup fish stock
1 preserved lemon, chopped
90g/3½oz/scant 1 cup black olives
60ml/4 tbsp chopped fresh coriander (cilantro), plus extra coriander leaves to garnish
couscous, to serve (*see* recipe, page 8)
salt and ground black pepper

1 Cut the fish into 5cm/2in chunks, then place the chunks in a wide bowl and add 30ml/2 tbsp of the harissa. Toss to coat, then cover and chill for at least 1 hour.

2 Heat half the olive oil in the base of a flameproof tagine or shallow heavy pan. Add the aubergine cubes and fry for about 10 minutes, or until they are golden brown. Add the courgette cubes and fry for 2 minutes more. Remove the vegetables using a slotted spoon and set aside.

3 Add the remaining olive oil to the tagine, then add the chopped onions and cook over a low heat for about 10 minutes, until golden brown. Stir in the remaining harissa and cook for 5 minutes more, stirring occasionally.

4 Put the courgette and aubergine back in the tagine, and stir to combine with the onions. Add the chopped tomatoes, passata and fish stock, and stir well. Bring to the boil, then lower the heat and simmer for about 20 minutes.

5 Add the marinated fish chunks, chopped preserved lemon and black olives to the pan, then stir gently so that you do not break up the delicate fish chunks. Cover the tagine with a lid and simmer over a low heat for about 15–20 minutes, or until the fish is cooked through.

6 Season to taste, then stir in the chopped fresh coriander. Serve immediately, accompanied by couscous, if you like, and garnished with some extra coriander leaves.

COOK'S TIP

To make this fish tagine go further, add 225g/8oz/1¼ cups cooked chickpeas to the tagine, which are delicious, filling and nutritious. If you choose to use dried chickpeas, you will need to soak them overnight, then boil them for 1–1½ hours, until soft. You can, however, use canned chickpeas, which are inexpensive and hassle-free.

Energy 263Kcal/1099kJ; Protein 32.3g; Carbohydrate 8.3g, of which sugars 7g; Fat 11.3g, of which saturates 1.7g; Cholesterol 75mg; Calcium 57mg; Fibre 3.2g; Sodium 360mg.

Tagine of monkfish, potatoes, cherry tomatoes and olives

The fish for this tagine is marinated in chermoula, which gives it that unmistakable Moroccan flavour. It is a delightful dish at any time of year, served with lots of crusty bread to mop up the tasty juices, but it is especially good made with flavourful new-season potatoes and sun-ripened cherry tomatoes.

SERVES 4

900g/2lb monkfish tail, cut into 5cm/2in chunks
90ml/6 tbsp chermoula (*see* recipe page 10 or use store-bought)
15–20 small new potatoes, scrubbed, scraped or peeled
45–60ml/3–4 tbsp olive oil
4–5 garlic cloves, thinly sliced
15–20 cherry tomatoes
2 green (bell) peppers, grilled (broiled) until black, skinned, seeded and cut into strips
a large handful of kalamata or fleshy black olives
100ml/3½fl oz/scant ½ cup water
salt and ground black pepper

1 Place the monkfish chunks in a bowl. Reserve a little chermoula for cooking, then rub the rest of the paste over the chunks of monkfish. Cover and leave to marinate for about 1 hour.

2 Par-boil the potatoes for 10 minutes, or until slightly softened. Drain, refresh under cold water and drain again, then cut them in half lengthways.

3 Heat the olive oil in a heavy pan and stir in the garlic. When the garlic begins to colour, add the tomatoes and cook until just softened. Add the peppers and the remaining chermoula, and season with salt and pepper.

4 Spread the potatoes over the base of a flameproof tagine, shallow pan or deep, ridged frying pan. Spoon three-quarters of the tomato and pepper mixture over and place the marinated fish chunks on top, with their marinade. Spoon the rest of the tomato and pepper mixture on top of the fish and add the olives. Drizzle a little extra olive oil over the dish and pour in the water.

5 Heat until simmering, then cover the tagine or pan with a lid and steam over a medium heat for about 15 minutes, or until the fish is cooked through. Serve immediately.

Energy 411kcal/1727kJ; Protein 41.2g; Carbohydrate 13.7g, of which sugars 3.9g; Fat 21.8g, of which saturates 2.1g; Cholesterol 60mg; Calcium 143mg; Fibre 4.3g; Sodium 821mg.

Baked fish tagine with lime and tomato salad

North African oven-baked tagines are very simple, often with the addition of a little bit of fruit or spice. This particular recipe is a delicious way of cooking red mullet as the flesh remains very moist. You can bake the fish in the shallow base of a tagine or in an earthenware baking dish.

SERVES 4

30ml/2 tbsp olive oil or argan oil
25g/1oz/2 tbsp butter
2–3 garlic cloves, finely sliced
4 red mullet, gutted and cleaned
2–3 limes, finely sliced
5–10ml/1–2 tsp sumac
a few fresh coriander (cilantro) leaves, to garnish
salt and ground black pepper

For the salad

4–6 ripe tomatoes, halved and finely sliced
2 green chillies, deseeded and finely sliced
15–30ml/1–2 tbsp olive oil or argan oil
salt and ground black pepper

1 Preheat the oven to 180°C/350°F/ Gas 4. Heat the oil and butter in a flameproof tagine or casserole, and stir in the garlic, until it begins to brown.

2 Remove from the heat, then place the fish in the tagine. Spoon some of the oil and garlic over the top, season with salt and pepper, and arrange the slices of lime over the top of each fish. Put the lid on the tagine, or cover with aluminium foil, and place it in the oven for 15 minutes.

3 Meanwhile, to make the salad, arrange the tomato slices in a shallow bowl. Sprinkle the chillies over the top, drizzle with a little oil, and season with salt and pepper. Set aside.

4 Remove the lid from the tagine, baste the fish with the cooking juices, and sprinkle over the sumac. Return the fish to the oven for 10 minutes. Garnish with some fresh coriander leaves, toss the tomato salad, and serve immediately.

VARIATIONS

Instead of red mullet, you can use other North African favourites, such as sardines, mackerel, red snapper, grouper or sea bass, and you can replace the lime with slices of lemon or bitter orange.

Energy 344kcal/1440kJ; Protein 39.1g; Carbohydrate 4.8g, of which sugars 4.8g; Fat 19.8g, of which saturates 1.8g; Cholesterol 0mg; Calcium 175mg; Fibre 2g; Sodium 199mg.

Fish and potato tagine with saffron and preserved lemon

Classic and simple, variations of this tagine can be found everywhere in Morocco – at the coast, in the mountains, in countryside villages – as it works well with both saltwater and freshwater fish, such as carp and trout. For depth of flavour, I like to roast the saffron first.

SERVES 4

500g/1lb 2oz new potatoes
a pinch of saffron fronds
150ml/¼ pint/⅔ cup warm water
juice of 2 lemons
45ml/3 tbsp olive oil
4–6 garlic cloves, peeled and smashed
4–6 medium tomatoes, finely sliced
1 preserved lemon, finely chopped
a small bunch of fresh flat leaf parsley, finely chopped
500g/1lb 2oz sea bass (or any firm-fleshed fish) fillets, cut into chunks
salt and ground black pepper
leafy green salad and couscous, to serve (*see* recipe, page 8)

COOK'S TIP

Saffron is an expensive ingredient, even in Morocco where it grows, so it is often replaced with the cheaper safflower, which imparts a similar colour but not the subtle, floral flavour.

1 Bring a pan of water to the boil. Add the potatoes and parboil them for 6–8 minutes, until just tender. Drain the potatoes, and refresh them in cold water. Peel off the skins, and cut them into 1cm/½in thick slices.

2 Prepare the saffron by dry-roasting the fronds in a small frying pan for less than a minute until they emit a faint aroma. Using a mortar and pestle, grind the fronds to a powder. Stir in the warm water until the saffron dissolves, then add the lemon juice and 30ml/2 tbsp of the olive oil. Set aside.

3 Heat the remaining olive oil in a flameproof tagine or casserole, and stir in the garlic. Cook for 1–2 minutes, until the garlic begins to colour.

4 Turn the heat to low and line the base of the tagine with a layer of potatoes, followed by a layer of tomatoes. Sprinkle half the preserved lemon and parsley over the tomatoes.

5 Arrange the fish on top, skin-side up, then pour the saffron liquid over the fish. Season with salt and pepper. Arrange the rest of the tomatoes, preserved lemon, and parsley on top.

6 Place the lid on the tagine and cook over a medium heat for 15–20 minutes, until the fish is just cooked and the flavours have mingled. Serve immediately with plain, buttery couscous and a leafy salad.

Energy 318kcal/1338kJ; Protein 28g; Carbohydrate 25.4g, of which sugars 5.9g; Fat 12.3g, of which saturates 1.9g; Cholesterol 141mg; Calcium 205mg; Fibre 4.5g; Sodium 116mg.

Prawn tagine with ginger and harissa couscous

This tasty prawn tagine from Tangier echoes some of the Andalucian flavours from across the water in Spain. It makes a filling main course, but you can also serve the prawn tagine without the couscous as a snack or appetizer with chunks of crusty bread to mop up the cooking juices.

SERVES 4

30ml/2 tbsp olive oil
2 onions, finely chopped
2 garlic cloves, finely chopped
50g/2oz fresh ginger, peeled and finely chopped
20 king prawns (jumbo shrimp), shells and heads removed
5–10ml/1–2 tsp sugar
5ml/1 tsp smoked paprika
1 x 400g/14oz tin of tomatoes, drained
125ml/4fl oz white wine or Fino sherry
a small bunch of fresh flat leaf parsley, finely chopped, plus some whole leaves to garnish
salt and ground black pepper

For the couscous

350g/12oz/2 cups couscous
2.5ml/½ tsp salt
400ml/14fl oz/1⅔ cups warm water
15–30ml/1–2 tbsp ghee, or olive oil with a knob of butter
10ml/2 tsp harissa
a small bunch of fresh coriander (cilantro), finely chopped

1 Place the couscous into an ovenproof dish. Stir the salt into the water and pour it over the couscous. Cover the couscous with a clean dish towel and leave it to absorb the water for 10–15 minutes.

2 Meanwhile, heat the olive oil in a flameproof tagine or casserole, and stir in the onions, garlic and ginger for 3–4 minutes, until they begin to colour.

3 Add the prawns, and cook until they turn opaque, then add the sugar, paprika, tomatoes, and wine. Bring to a simmer, then cover with the lid, and cook over a gentle heat for 15 minutes.

4 Using a fork, rake through the couscous to separate the grains. Heat the ghee, or olive oil and butter, in the base of a tagine or wide shallow pan, and stir in the harissa paste. Add the couscous, and stir until well mixed. Season with salt and pepper, and stir in the fresh coriander.

VARIATION

This tagine works well using scallops, or a combination of prawns and scallops. You can also serve the tagine with couscous combined with chopped herbs and preserved lemon instead of the harissa.

5 Season the tagine with salt and pepper, stir in the chopped parsley, then garnish with the leaves. Serve immediately with the harissa couscous.

Energy 428kcal/1795kJ; Protein 28.2g; Carbohydrate 46.7g, of which sugars 6.6g; Fat 13.3g, of which saturates 1.9g; Cholesterol 263mg; Calcium 205mg; Fibre 3g; Sodium 1553mg.

Mixed seafood tagine

The distinctive mixture of spices and chillies used here is similar to a classic chermoula. Scorpion fish is the traditional choice for this dish, and red mullet or snapper makes a good, authentic alternative, but you can substitute other fish – try red bream, pomfret, porgy or even halved cod or hake steaks.

SERVES 4

60ml/4 tbsp olive oil
4 garlic cloves, sliced
1–2 green chillies, seeded and chopped
a large handful of fresh flat leaf parsley, roughly chopped
5ml/1 tsp coriander seeds
2.5ml/½ tsp ground allspice
6 cardamom pods, split open
2.5ml/½ tsp ground turmeric
15ml/1 tbsp lemon juice
350g/12oz scorpion fish, red mullet or red snapper fillets, cut into large chunks
225g/8oz squid, cleaned and cut into rings
1 onion, chopped
4 tomatoes, seeded and chopped
300ml/½ pint/1¼ cups warm fish or vegetable stock
225g/8oz king prawns (jumbo shrimp)
15ml/1 tbsp chopped fresh coriander (cilantro)
salt and ground black pepper
lemon wedges, to garnish
couscous, to serve (*see* recipe, page 8)

1 Place the olive oil, garlic, chillies, parsley, coriander seeds, allspice and cardamom pods in a mortar and pound to a smooth paste using a pestle. Stir in the ground turmeric and lemon juice, and season with salt and pepper.

2 Place the chunks of fish in a large bowl with the squid rings. Add the spice paste and toss together. Cover and leave the fish to marinate in the refrigerator for at least 2 hours, or longer, if time allows.

3 Place the chopped onion, seeded and chopped tomatoes and stock in a tagine or casserole, and cover with a lid or aluminium foil. Place the tagine in an unheated oven, then set the temperature to 200°C/400°F/Gas 6. Cook for 20 minutes.

4 Remove the fish from the marinade, then drain well. Set aside the squid and any excess marinade, then place the fish in the tagine with the vegetables. Cover and cook for 5 minutes more.

5 Add the prawns, squid rings and the remaining marinade to the tagine, and stir gently to combine, being careful not to break up the fish. Cover the tagine and return it to the oven for 5–10 minutes, or until all the fish, prawns and squid are cooked through.

6 Taste the sauce and season with salt and pepper if necessary, then stir in most of the chopped fresh coriander. Serve immediately, garnished with lemon wedges and the rest of the chopped fresh coriander, accompanied by couscous.

COOK'S TIP

To ensure that the fish fillets have no tiny bones left in the flesh after filleting, lay the fillets on a board, skin-side down, and run your hand gently over the surface of the flesh, to feel for bones. Pull out any bones you find using a pair of tweezers.

Energy 301Kcal/1261kJ; Protein 37.2g; Carbohydrate 7.1g, of which sugars 5.5g; Fat 14g, of which saturates 2.2g; Cholesterol 269mg; Calcium 128mg; Fibre 2.2g; Sodium 251mg.

Shellfish k'dra with lemon couscous

Shellfish k'dras are a lovely feature of the busy fishing ports in Tangier, Casablanca and Essaouira, where you can sit outdoors and enjoy the day's catch in one pot. In a traditional home, a shellfish k'dra would be prepared for a special occasion, such as a family celebration or religious feast.

SERVES 6–8

For the k'dra

45ml/3 tbsp olive oil or argan oil
10ml/2 tsp coriander seeds
10ml/2 tsp fennel seeds
2–3 red chillies, deseeded and finely chopped
5–10ml/1–2 tsp sugar
10ml/2 tsp ground turmeric
2 x 400g/14oz cans of tomatoes, drained of juice
300ml/½ pint/1¼ cups white wine
1.2 litres/2 pints/5 cups fish stock
4 garlic cloves, finely sliced
a small bunch of fresh flat leaf parsley, finely chopped
a small bunch of fresh coriander (cilantro), finely chopped
300g/10oz prawns (shrimp), shelled and deveined
300g/10oz mussels, thoroughly cleaned in a bowl of cold water (discard any that do not close when tapped on the work surface)
450g/1lb scallops, shelled and cleaned
salt and ground black pepper

For the couscous

800g/1¾lb/4½ cups couscous
900ml/1½ pints/3¾ cups warm water
2.5ml/½ tsp salt
30ml/2 tbsp sunflower oil
1 preserved lemon, finely chopped
a small bunch of fresh flat leaf parsley, finely chopped
a small bunch of fresh mint, finely chopped
ground black pepper
25g/1oz/2 tbsp butter

1 Preheat the oven to 180°C/350°F/ Gas 4. Place the couscous in an ovenproof dish. Mix the water and salt, then pour over the couscous. Cover and leave for 10–15 minutes, until the couscous has swollen.

2 Meanwhile, heat the olive or argan oil in a large copper, or heavy, pan. Add the coriander seeds, fennel seeds, chillies and sugar, and stir for 2 minutes until fragrant. Stir in the turmeric, then add the drained tomatoes with the wine and fish stock. Add the garlic and most of the herbs, reserving the rest for garnishing, and bring to the boil. Reduce the heat and simmer for 15 minutes.

3 Meanwhile, using your fingers, rub the sunflower oil into the couscous to separate the grains, then rub in the preserved lemon. Stir in the herbs, and season with a little black pepper.

4 Cut the butter into pieces, and sprinkle over the top of the couscous, then cover with a dampened piece of baking parchment. Bake the couscous in the oven for 15–20 minutes to heat through.

5 Season the stock with salt and pepper and bring it to the boil again. Stir in the prawns, mussels and scallops, and cook over a medium heat for about 10 minutes, or until the shellfish is cooked through. Discard any mussels that have not opened.

6 Pile the couscous in a mound on a shallow serving dish. Hollow out the top of the dome and, using a slotted spoon, place most of the shellfish in the hollow and around the edge of the dish. Drizzle a little of the stock over the shellfish to keep it moist and pour the rest into a bowl to serve with it. Garnish with the reserved fresh parsley and coriander.

COOK'S TIPS

- A k'dra is a big copper pot, and the idea of using one is to cook for a larger quantity of people than a tagine can cater for. However, if you want to make a smaller amount, simply halve the quantities, and cook the same recipe in a tagine.
- To devein a prawn, use a sharp knife to make a shallow incision down the curved back, then remove the black vein.

Energy 447kcal/1870kJ; Protein 30.9g; Carbohydrate 56.2g, of which sugars 2g; Fat 12.8g, of which saturates 3g; Cholesterol 122mg; Calcium 129mg; Fibre 0.8g; Sodium 308mg.

Poultry

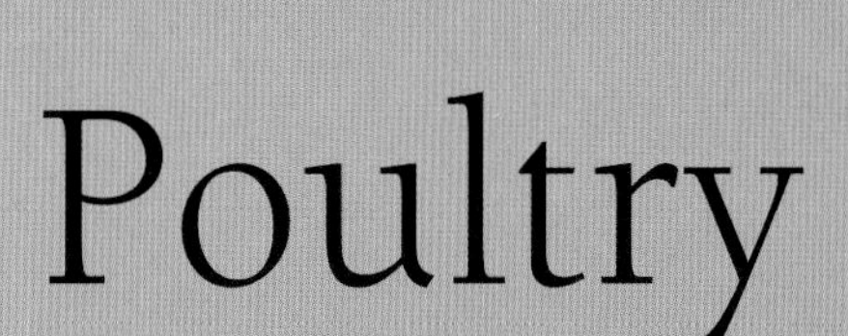

Chicken is a popular base for tagines, and both breasts and thighs lend themselves to this cooking method. Duck is also put to good use in traditional and modern tagines, as its succulent flesh and bold flavour hold their own in the spices and seasonings of Moroccan cooking. Whether you want to cook chicken breasts, duck legs or little poussins or even a whole chicken, there is plenty of inspiration here.

Chicken tagine with green olives and preserved lemon

This dish, which is particularly enjoyed in Marrakesh, celebrates two of Morocco's most famous ingredients – cracked green olives and preserved lemons. Try this recipe when you are looking for a new way to cook a whole chicken instead of by the usual roasting method. Serve simply with a pile of plain couscous and a leafy green salad.

SERVES 4

1.3kg/3lb chicken
3 garlic cloves, crushed
a small bunch of fresh coriander (cilantro), finely chopped
juice of ½ lemon
5ml/1 tsp coarse salt
45–60ml/3–4 tbsp olive oil
1 large onion, grated
pinch of saffron threads
5ml/1 tsp ground ginger
5ml/1 tsp ground black pepper
1 cinnamon stick
175g/6oz/1½ cups cracked green olives
2 preserved lemons, cut into strips
couscous, to serve (*see* recipe, page 8)

1 Place the chicken in a deep dish. Rub the garlic, coriander, lemon juice and salt into the body cavity of the chicken. Mix the olive oil with the grated onion, saffron, ginger and pepper and rub this mixture over the outside of the chicken. Cover and leave to stand for about 30 minutes.

2 Transfer the chicken to a flameproof tagine or casserole, and pour the marinating juices over. Pour in enough water to come halfway up the chicken, then add the cinnamon stick and bring the water to the boil. Reduce the heat, cover with a lid and simmer for 1 hour, turning the chicken occasionally.

3 Preheat the oven to 150°C/300°F/Gas 2. Using two slotted spoons, carefully lift the chicken out of the tagine or casserole and set aside on a plate, covered with foil.

4 Turn up the heat and boil the cooking liquid for 5 minutes to reduce it. Place the chicken back into the liquid, and baste it thoroughly.

5 Add the olives and strips of preserved lemon, then place the tagine or casserole in the oven for 15 minutes, until the chicken is cooked through. Serve the chicken, olives and lemon immediately, on a bed of couscous.

Energy 597kcal/2471kJ; Protein 41.8g; Carbohydrate 5.3g, of which sugars 3.8g; Fat 45.4g, of which saturates 10.5g; Cholesterol 215mg; Calcium 80mg; Fibre 3.7g; Sodium 1137mg.

Chicken tagine with apricots, rosemary, ginger and harissa

Fruity and spicy, with the delightful aroma of rosemary and sweetened ginger, this is the type of tagine best served with bread to mop up all the delectable syrupy juices. Served with a fresh leafy or crunchy vegetable salad, it is a perfect introduction to the flavours of Morocco.

SERVES 4

15–30ml/1–2 tbsp ghee or argan oil
1 onion, finely chopped
15ml/1 tbsp finely chopped rosemary
15–30ml/1–2 tbsp finely chopped preserved stem ginger
5–10ml/1–2 tsp harissa (*see* recipe, page 11, or use store-bought)
8 skinless chicken thighs
175g/6oz ready-to-eat dried apricots
2 sprigs rosemary
juice of 1 lemon
1 lemon, cut into quarters
30ml/2 tbsp clear honey
salt and ground black pepper
a small bunch of fresh green or purple basil leaves, to garnish
crusty bread and a leafy green salad, to serve

1 Heat the ghee in the base of a flameproof tagine or casserole, and add the onion. Cook, stirring, for 1–2 minutes to soften. Add the chopped rosemary and preserved stem ginger, and cook for 1–2 minutes, until fragrant, then stir in the harissa.

2 Add the chicken thighs, coating them in the onion mixture, and add the apricots with the sprigs of rosemary. Pour in enough water to cover the base of the tagine and come halfway up the chicken thighs. Pour in the lemon juice and slip in the lemon quarters. Drizzle the honey over the tagine, put on the lid, and cook the tagine over a gentle heat for about 45 minutes, adding more water if necessary.

3 Season the dish with salt and pepper, and garnish with the fresh basil leaves. Serve immediately, with chunks of crusty bread to dip into the syrupy cooking juices.

VARIATIONS

- As an alternative to chicken thighs, you could adapt the recipe to use breasts of chicken, pigeon, turkey, pheasant or duck, and serve the tagine with couscous.
- For a dinner party or special occasion, you could add white wine to the tagine in step 2 instead of water, or use a mixture.

Energy 377kcal/1582kJ; Protein 44g; Carbohydrate 20.9g, of which sugars 19.6g; Fat 13.6g, of which saturates 5.2g; Cholesterol 210mg; Calcium 68mg; Fibre 4.3g; Sodium 188mg.

Chicken tagine with courgettes, lemon and mint

This is one of the lovely, light summery tagines I came across in the agricultural regions of Morocco, as well as in the rich mountainous pastures. What is actually cooked in the tagine varies according to the harvest of the region, but the tagine should always be tangy and flavoured with herbs.

SERVES 4–6

30ml/2 tbsp olive oil or argan oil
1 onion, finely chopped
2–3 garlic cloves, finely chopped
2 red chillies, deseeded and finely chopped
10ml/2 tsp coriander seeds
5ml/1 tsp cumin seeds
5ml/1 tsp dried mint
4 chicken breasts, cut into bitesize pieces
juice of 1 lemon
1 lemon, cut into 4–6 wedges
2 courgettes (zucchini), sliced thickly on the diagonal
4 tomatoes, peeled, seeded and cut into chunks
a small bunch of fresh flat leaf parsley, roughly chopped
a small bunch of fresh mint, roughly chopped
salt and ground black pepper
couscous, to serve (*see* recipe, page 8)

1 Heat the oil in the base of a flameproof tagine or casserole, and stir in the onion, garlic, chillies, coriander and cumin seeds. Cook for 2–3 minutes. Add the dried mint and chicken, stirring to coat it in the onion and spices.

2 Add the lemon juice and lemon wedges, and pour in enough water to cover the base of the tagine. Bring the water to the boil, then put the lid on the tagine, turn the heat down to low, and simmer the chicken for 35 minutes.

3 Season the cooking juices with salt and pepper. Add the courgettes and tomatoes. Add most of the chopped fresh parsley and mint, reserving a little for the garnish. Top up the water, if necessary. Put the lid back on and cook gently for 10–15 minutes, until the courgettes are cooked but still have a slight bite to them.

4 Garnish with the reserved herbs, and serve with couscous.

VARIATIONS

You can vary this summer tagine with peas, green beans, broad (fava) beans, and aubergines (eggplants). Try lamb instead of chicken, increasing the cooking time for tender results.

Energy 154kcal/645kJ; Protein 22.6g; Carbohydrate 5g, of which sugars 4.4g; Fat 6.1g, of which saturates 0.9g; Cholesterol 58mg; Calcium 78mg; Fibre 2.5g; Sodium 62mg.

Chicken k'dra with turnip and ras el hanout

This rustic dish, cooked in a traditional copper pot, is designed to feed a big family or a group of people gathered together for a celebratory occasion. From Meknes to Marrakesh, every Moroccan village has its own variation of this k'dra, but the recipe given here is a classic one.

SERVES 6–8

30–45ml/2–3 tbsp smen or ghee
4 onions, finely chopped
4 garlic cloves, finely chopped
10ml/2 tsp cumin seeds
16 chicken thighs, skinned
10–15ml/2–3 tsp ras el hanout (*see* recipe, page 11, or use store-bought)
10ml/2 tsp sugar
2 x 400g/14oz cans chopped tomatoes
1.2 litres/2 pints/5 cups chicken stock
500g/1lb 2oz peeled turnip flesh, cut into bitesize chunks
a bunch of fresh coriander (cilantro), coarsely chopped
a bunch of fresh flat leaf parsley, coarsely chopped
15ml/1 tbsp butter
salt and ground black pepper
couscous, to serve (*see* recipe, page 8)

1 Heat the smen or ghee in a large copper, or heavy, pan. Stir in the onions, garlic and cumin seeds, and cook for 2–3 minutes. Add the chicken thighs, stir to coat them in the onion mixture, then cook until lightly browned.

2 Add the ras el hanout, followed by the sugar and tomatoes, then pour in the stock. Bring the liquid to the boil, then reduce the heat, put on the lid, and cook gently for 45 minutes.

3 Add the turnip, and top up the liquid with a little water, if necessary. Cook for 15 minutes, or until the turnip is tender.

4 Season the k'dra with salt and pepper, and add half the fresh herbs. Melt the butter in a small pan, and drizzle it on to the surface of the k'dra. Garnish with the rest of the fresh coriander and parsley, and serve with a mound of couscous, or chunks of crusty bread to mop up the sauce.

VARIATIONS

For a Spanish-influenced version of this k'dra, you can combine the chicken with thickly sliced, spicy merguez or chorizo sausage. You can also combine the chicken with prawns (shrimp), and substitute the turnip with pumpkin or butternut squash.

Energy 322kcal/1348kJ; Protein 43.7g; Carbohydrate 12.2g, of which sugars 9.8g; Fat 11.3g, of which saturates 4.4g; Cholesterol 214mg; Calcium 73mg; Fibre 3.9g; Sodium 205mg.

Chicken k'dra with chickpeas and almonds

A k'dra is traditionally cooked with smen, a strongly flavoured clarified butter, and plenty of onions. The almonds in this recipe are pre-cooked until soft, adding an interesting texture and flavour to the lightly spiced chicken. Saffron is expensive, but you need only a tiny amount.

SERVES 4

- 75g/3oz/½ cup blanched almonds
- 75g/3oz/½ cup chickpeas, soaked overnight and drained
- 4 part-boned skinless chicken breast portions
- 50g/2oz/¼ cup butter
- 2.5ml/½ tsp saffron threads
- 2 Spanish (Bermuda) onions, thinly sliced
- 900ml/1½ pints/3¾ cups chicken stock
- 1 small cinnamon stick
- 60ml/4 tbsp chopped fresh flat leaf parsley, plus extra to garnish
- lemon juice, to taste
- salt and ground black pepper

1 Place the almonds in a pan of water and simmer for 1½–2 hours until fairly soft, then drain and set aside.

2 Meanwhile, cook the chickpeas in a pan of boiling water for 1–1½ hours until they are completely soft. Drain, then place in a bowl of cold water and rub with your fingers to remove the skins. Discard the skins and drain.

3 Place the chicken portions in a flameproof tagine or heavy pan, together with the butter and half of the saffron, and season with salt and plenty of black pepper. Heat gently, stirring, until the butter has melted.

4 Add the onions and stock, bring to the boil and then add the chickpeas and cinnamon stick. Cover and cook very gently for 45–60 minutes.

5 Transfer the chicken to a serving plate and keep warm. Bring the sauce to the boil and simmer until reduced, stirring frequently.

6 Add the almonds, parsley and the remaining saffron, and cook for 2–3 minutes.

7 Sharpen the sauce with a little lemon juice, then pour the sauce over the chicken. Serve, garnished with extra parsley.

Energy 477Kcal/1994kJ; Protein 46g; Carbohydrate 21g, of which sugars 8.7g; Fat 23.9g, of which saturates 7.9g; Cholesterol 132mg; Calcium 146mg; Fibre 5.9g; Sodium 185mg.

Tagine of poussins with dates and orange flower water

Dates and almonds are probably the most ancient culinary combination in Arab cuisines, married in sweet dishes or with lamb and chicken. For this type of tagine, the small birds can be cooked on top of the stove or in the oven. Quail, partridge, pheasant or pigeon can be used instead of poussins, if you like. Served with a salad and couscous, this makes a lovely dinner party dish.

SERVES 4

25g/1oz fresh root ginger, peeled and roughly chopped
2 garlic cloves
60ml/4 tbsp olive oil
juice of 1 lemon
30–45ml/2–3 tbsp clear honey
4 small poussins
350g/12oz/2 cups moist dried dates, pitted
5–10ml/1–2 tsp ground cinnamon
15ml/1 tbsp orange flower water
knob (pat) of butter
45ml/3 tbsp flaked (sliced) almonds
salt and ground black pepper
fresh coriander (cilantro), to garnish

1 Using a mortar and pestle, crush the ginger with the garlic to form a paste. Mix the paste with the olive oil, lemon juice and honey, and season with salt and pepper.

2 Place the poussins in a flameproof tagine or casserole and rub the paste all over them. Pour in a little water to cover the base of the dish and bring to the boil. Reduce the heat, cover with a lid, and simmer for about 30 minutes, turning the poussins occasionally, until they are cooked through. Top up the water during cooking, if necessary.

3 Lift the poussins out of the tagine, transfer them to a plate, cover with foil and keep hot. Add the dates to the liquid in the tagine and stir in the cinnamon and orange flower water. Cook gently for 10 minutes, or until the dates are soft and have absorbed the flavours of the sauce, as well as some of the liquid.

4 Replace the poussins and cover the tagine to keep hot. Melt the butter in a separate pan, add the almonds and cook until lightly browned. Sprinkle the almonds them over the poussins, and serve immediately, garnished with some fresh coriander leaves.

Energy 670kcal/2810kJ; Protein 27.3g; Carbohydrate 68.9g, of which sugars 67.6g; Fat 33.7g, of which saturates 7.7g; Cholesterol 121mg; Calcium 68mg; Fibre 4.4g; Sodium 106mg.

Tagine of duck with chestnuts and pomegranate seeds

This is a lovely aromatic, winter dish, decorated with ruby-red pomegranate seeds – ideal for seasonal celebrations. Whole chestnuts are sometimes used in Arab-influenced dishes as a substitute for potatoes, as they are quite filling and can be found in abundance in the colder months.

SERVES 4

30ml/2 tbsp ghee
2 onions, finely chopped
4 garlic cloves, finely chopped
25g/1oz fresh ginger, finely chopped
10ml/2 tsp cumin seeds
2–3 dried red chillies, left whole
4 duck legs
600ml/1 pint/2½ cups chicken stock
300g/10oz shelled chestnuts
30ml/2 tbsp honey
salt and ground black pepper
seeds of 1 pomegranate, with the pith removed
a small bunch of fresh mint leaves, finely chopped
a small bunch of fresh coriander (cilantro), finely chopped
couscous, to serve (*see* recipe, page 8)

1 Heat the ghee in the base of a flameproof tagine or shallow heavy pan, and stir in the onions, garlic, ginger, and cumin seeds. Cook for 2–3 minutes, until they begin to colour.

2 Add the dried chillies and duck legs. Pour in the chicken stock and bring it to the boil. Reduce the heat, cover with a lid, and simmer gently for 25–30 minutes.

3 Add the chestnuts and honey, put the lid back on, and cook gently for a further 25–30 minutes, until the chicken is very tender.

4 Season with salt and plenty of black pepper, and add most of the pomegranate seeds, fresh mint and fresh coriander, reserving some for the garnish. Cook for 5–10 minutes more.

5 Garnish with the reserved pomegranate seeds and herbs, and serve the tagine with couscous.

COOK'S TIP

You can use vacuum-packed peeled chestnuts, frozen peeled chestnuts, or freshly roasted chestnuts, which are easy to shell. If you can't find chestnuts, you can substitute them with small, peeled potatoes.

Energy 614kcal/2575kJ; Protein 53.1g; Carbohydrate 44.9g, of which sugars 19.9g; Fat 26.6g, of which saturates 9.1g; Cholesterol 275mg; Calcium 136mg; Fibre 7.7g; Sodium 295mg.

Duck tagine with saffron, caramelized pears and orange salad

Duck and pigeon tagines are popular in the cities of Fes and Marrakesh, and very often they are combined with fruit in the style of medieval Arab recipes. In my home, we prepare this dish for festive occasions, and it is best served with a mound of plain, buttery couscous and a fruity salad.

SERVES 4

500g/1lb 2oz duck breasts
30ml/2 tbsp olive oil or argan oil
2 onions, finely chopped
25g/1oz fresh ginger, peeled and finely chopped
2–3 cinnamon sticks
a fingerful of saffron threads, soaked in 30ml/2 tbsp water
300ml/½ pint/1¼ cups chicken stock
150ml/¼ pint/⅔ cup white wine
30ml/2 tbsp butter
2 pears, peeled, quartered and cored
30ml/2 tbsp honey
30–45ml/2–3 tbsp orange blossom water
salt and ground black pepper
a small bunch of fresh flat leaf parsley, finely chopped
couscous, to serve (*see* recipe, page 8)

For the orange salad

2–3 oranges
15–30ml/1–2 tbsp orange blossom water
1 green chilli, finely sliced

1 Slice the duck breasts into thick strips. Heat the oil in the base of a flameproof tagine or casserole, and stir in the onions and ginger. Cook for 2–3 minutes, until they begin to colour. Add the cinnamon sticks and duck, turning the duck to make sure it is coated in the ginger and onions.

2 Stir in the saffron and its soaking water, chicken stock and wine. Bring the liquid to the boil, then reduce the heat, put on the lid, and cook the duck over a low heat for 25–30 minutes.

3 Meanwhile, melt the butter in a heavy pan, then add the pears, and cook for 2–3 minutes. Add the honey, and continue to cook until the pears begin to caramelize.

4 Add the caramelized pears to the tagine along with the orange blossom water. Season, then put the lid back on, and cook gently for 10–15 minutes, to allow the flavours to mingle.

5 To prepare the salad, peel the oranges with a small, sharp knife, removing the skin and pith. Cut the oranges horizontally into thin slices, remove any pips, and arrange them in a shallow serving dish. Sprinkle the orange blossom water over them, and arrange the sliced chillies over the top.

6 When ready to serve, toss the salad. Garnish the tagine with the parsley, and serve with a mound of buttery couscous, and accompanied by the orange salad.

VARIATIONS

Although this dish is particularly festive prepared with duck, you can easily alter it by using chicken, turkey, or pigeon breasts instead. Equally, you can substitute the pears with quinces and serve it with a zingy, fruity salad with grapefruit.

Energy 404kcal/1691kJ; Protein 26.6g; Carbohydrate 24.8g, of which sugars 24.3g; Fat 20.2g, of which saturates 7.2g; Cholesterol 154mg; Calcium 89mg; Fibre 5g; Sodium 317mg.

Meat

When you think of tagines, you often think of lamb, slow-cooked in earthy spices to tender perfection. This chapter showcases some of North Africa's finest lamb tagines, as well as introducing recipes that have other meats as the star of the show. Beef is a favourite for special occasions, and spicy sausages pack a punch. Whether it is for a whole leg of lamb stewed for hours or quick-cooking kefta, there is a recipe here for every occasion.

Black-eyed bean stew with spicy sausage

Bean stews made with spicy cured sausage are popular in the Middle East and North Africa. I used black-eyed beans here, but any beans or chickpeas may be substituted. Accompany this with a salad of hot green peppers and parsley, or pickled vegetables.

SERVES 4–6

175g/6oz/scant 1 cup dried black-eyed beans (peas), soaked in cold water overnight
30ml/2 tbsp ghee or 15ml/1 tbsp each olive oil and butter
1 large onion, cut in half lengthways and sliced along the grain
2–3 garlic cloves, roughly chopped and bruised with the flat side of a knife
5ml/1 tsp cumin seeds
5–10ml/1–2 tsp coriander seeds
5ml/1 tsp fennel seeds
5–10ml/1–2 tsp sugar or clear honey
1 spicy cured sausage, about 25cm/10in long, sliced
150ml/¼ pint/⅔ cup white wine
400g/14oz can tomatoes
a bunch of fresh flat leaf parsley, roughly chopped
salt and ground black pepper
salad, to serve

1 Drain the soaked black-eyed beans, transfer them to a pan and fill the pan with plenty of cold water. Bring to the boil and boil for 1 minute, then lower the heat and partially cover the pan with a lid. Simmer the beans for about 25 minutes, or until they are tender but retain a little bite.

2 Drain the beans, then rinse well under cold running water and remove any loose skins.

3 Preheat the oven to 180°C/350°F/Gas 4. Melt the ghee in a flameproof tagine or casserole. Stir in the onion, garlic and spices, and fry until the onion begins to colour.

4 Stir in the sugar or honey, add in the spicy sausage, and cook until it begins to brown.

5 Add the beans, followed by the wine, and stir. Bring to the boil to boil off the alcohol, then lower the heat and add the tomatoes. Stir in half the parsley, and season with salt and pepper.

6 Cover with a lid and bake for about 40 minutes. Before serving, adjust the seasoning to taste and sprinkle with the remaining parsley. Serve with a salad on the side.

COOK'S TIP

This tagine has a Middle Eastern feel to it, and you can use a Turkish, Greek or Italian spicy sausage here for good flavour. The Turkish sucuk is a good choice – it is horseshoe-shaped and spiked with cumin.

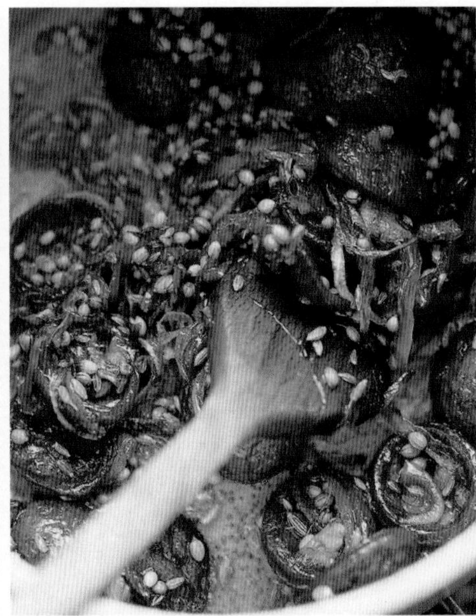

Energy 382kcal/1594kJ; Protein 18g; Carbohydrate 20g, of which sugars 6.7g; Fat 24.4g, of which saturates 10g; Cholesterol 52mg; Calcium 55mg; Fibre 6g; Sodium 944mg.

Tagine of spiced kefta with lemon and spices

The kefta, or meatballs, are poached gently with lemon and spices to make a dish that is surprisingly light. Serve it with a salad for lunch. In Morocco today, this dish is found in the tiniest rural villages, in street stalls in the towns and cities, or in the finest restaurants of Casablanca, Fes and Marrakesh.

SERVES 4

450g/1lb finely minced (ground) lamb
3 large onions, grated
a small bunch of fresh flat leaf parsley, chopped
5–10ml/1–2 tsp ground cinnamon
5ml/1 tsp ground cumin
a pinch of cayenne pepper
40g/1¼oz/3 tbsp butter
25g/1oz fresh root ginger, peeled and finely chopped
1 hot chilli, seeded and finely chopped
a pinch of saffron threads
juice of 1 lemon
a small bunch of fresh coriander (cilantro), finely chopped
300ml/½ pint/1¼ cups water
1 lemon, quartered
salt and ground black pepper
salad and crusty bread, to serve

1 To make the kefta, pound the minced lamb in a bowl by using your hand to lift it up and slap it back down into the bowl. Knead in half the grated onions, the parsley, cinnamon, cumin and cayenne pepper. Season with salt and pepper, and continue pounding the mixture by hand for a few minutes, until well combined.

2 Break off pieces of the mixture, and shape them into walnut-sized balls.

3 In a flameproof tagine or heavy lidded frying pan, melt the butter and add the remaining onion with the ginger, chilli and saffron. Stirring frequently, cook just until the onion begins to colour, then stir in the lemon juice and most of the coriander.

4 Pour in the water, season with salt and bring to the boil.

5 Drop in the kefta, reduce the heat and cover the pan. Poach the kefta gently, turning them occasionally, for about 20 minutes.

6 Remove the lid from the tagine or pan, tuck the lemon quarters around the kefta and cook, uncovered, for a further 10 minutes, to reduce the liquid slightly.

7 Garnish the kefta with the rest of the chopped coriander. Serve hot, straight from the pan, accompanied by a leafy salad and with plenty of crusty fresh bread to mop up the delicious juices.

Energy 362Kcal/1503kJ; Protein 24.5g; Carbohydrate 12.9g, of which sugars 9.3g; Fat 24g, of which saturates 12.2g; Cholesterol 108mg; Calcium 134mg; Fibre 4g; Sodium 155mg.

Tagine of baked lamb with chermoula, figs and honey

This traditional Berber dish is generally prepared for religious feasts and family celebrations. It can be adapted to cook a whole lamb or goat over a camp fire, as well as a leg or shoulder that will fit into a wide tagine base or an earthenware baking dish. The meat is cooked slowly so that it is very tender.

SERVES 4–8

- roughly 1.5kg/3lb 5oz leg or shoulder of lamb on the bone
- 90ml/6 tbsp chermoula (*see* recipe, page 10, or use store-bought)
- 30ml/2 tbsp ghee
- 2 red onions, halved lengthways and sliced with the grain
- 6 fresh figs, halved or quartered
- 25g/1oz butter, cut into little pieces
- 30–45ml/2–3 tbsp orange flower water
- 30ml/2 tbsp clear honey
- salt and ground black pepper
- a small bunch of fresh flat leaf parsley, roughly chopped
- a small bunch of fresh coriander (cilantro), roughly chopped

1 Preheat the oven to 180°C/350°F/Gas 4. Using a small sharp knife, cut small incisions in the lamb and rub the chermoula all over the meat, working the mixture well into the incisions. Cover and marinate in the refrigerator for at least 6 hours, or overnight.

2 Heat the ghee in a wide flameproof tagine or casserole, and add the onions. Cook for 2–3 minutes, stirring, to soften.

VARIATIONS

- Fresh figs look particularly attractive, but, if you can't get fresh figs, use fresh halved and stoned apricots, or dried figs or dates.
- A festive dish like this would normally be eaten on its own and then followed by a giant mound of couscous, but it is also good served with potatoes and vegetables.

3 Place the leg of lamb in the onions and brown it lightly on all sides.

4 Pour in 300ml/½ pint/1¼ cups water and mix it well with the onions and chermoula. Cover the tagine and place it in the oven for about 2 hours, basting from time to time.

5 Take the tagine out of the oven, place the figs around the lamb and dot them with the butter. Splash the orange flower water over the lamb, and drizzle the honey over the meat and figs. Season the lamb with salt and pepper and return it, uncovered, to the oven for about 30 minutes, until the lamb is nicely browned and tender.

6 Let the lamb rest for about 10–15 minutes before serving, then garnish with the parsley and coriander. Serve with a salad, couscous or potatoes and steamed vegetables.

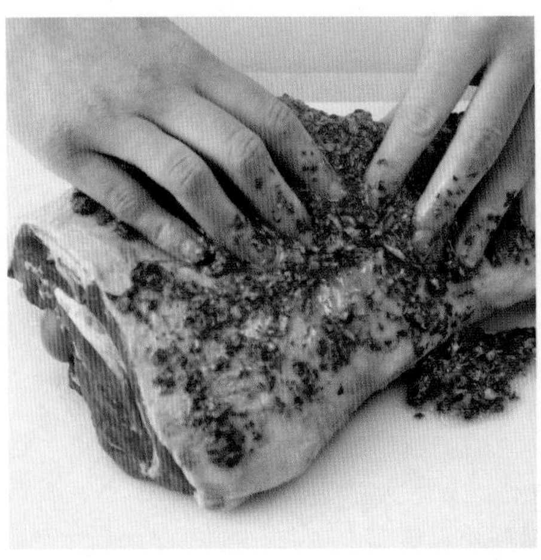

Energy 453kcal/1902kJ; Protein 56.7g; Carbohydrate 8.8g, of which sugars 7.6g; Fat 21.6g, of which saturates 9g; Cholesterol 188mg; Calcium 46mg; Fibre 1.7g; Sodium 123mg.

Tagine of lamb with crunchy country salad

Morocco's hearty tagines are well known for their succulent meat cooked in a combination of honey and warm spices. This delicious recipe is for one of the most traditional and popular tagines, which is best served with a crunchy salad, spiked with chilli to balance the sweetness of the main dish. Offer lots of fresh bread for mopping up the thick, syrupy sauce.

SERVES 6

1kg/2¼lb boneless shoulder of lamb, trimmed and cubed
30–45ml/2–3 tbsp sunflower oil
25g/1oz fresh root ginger, peeled and chopped
a pinch of saffron threads
10ml/2 tsp ground cinnamon
1 onion, finely chopped
2–3 garlic cloves, chopped
350g/12oz/1½ cups pitted prunes, soaked for 1 hour
30ml/2 tbsp clear honey
salt and ground black pepper
flatbread, to serve

For the salad

2 onions, chopped
1 red (bell) pepper, seeded and chopped
1 green (bell) pepper, seeded and chopped
2–3 celery sticks, chopped
2–3 green chillies, seeded and chopped
2 garlic cloves, chopped
30ml/2 tbsp olive oil
juice of ½ lemon
a small bunch of fresh flat leaf parsley, chopped
a little fresh mint, chopped

1 Put the lamb in the base of a flameproof tagine or casserole. Add the oil, ginger, saffron, cinnamon, onion, garlic and seasoning, then pour in enough water to cover. Heat until just simmering, then cover with a lid and simmer gently for about 2 hours, topping up the water if necessary, until the meat is very tender.

2 Drain the prunes and add them to the tagine. Stir in the honey and simmer for a further 30 minutes, or until the sauce has reduced.

3 To make the salad, mix the onions, peppers, celery, chillies and garlic in a bowl. Pour the olive oil and lemon juice over the vegetables and toss to coat. Season with salt and add the parsley and mint.

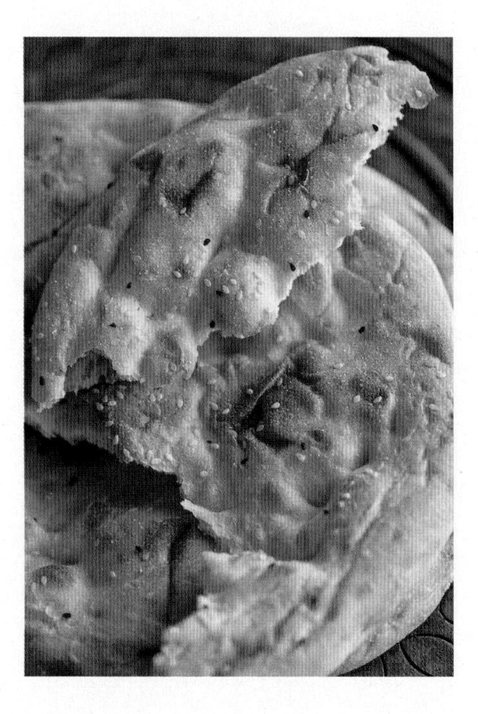

4 Serve the hot lamb tagine with the chilli-laced salad, and some bread for mopping up the juices.

Energy 600kcal/2504kJ; Protein 42g; Carbohydrate 28.2g, of which sugars 25.8g; Fat 36.3g, of which saturates 10.9g; Cholesterol 222mg; Calcium 112mg; Fibre 4.9g; Sodium 199mg.

Tagine of lamb with prunes

This delicious tagine combines sweetness from prunes and honey, warmth from ginger and cinnamon, and a little crunch from toasted almonds. To serve, prepare some couscous, then stir in some finely chopped fresh coriander for extra flavour and colour.

SERVES 6

1kg/2¼lb lean boneless lamb, such as shoulder or neck fillet
25g/1oz/2 tbsp butter
15ml/1 tbsp sunflower oil
1 large onion, chopped
2 garlic cloves, chopped
2.5cm/1in piece fresh root ginger, peeled and finely chopped
1 red (bell) pepper, seeded and chopped
900ml/1½ pints/3¾ cups lamb stock or water
250g/9oz ready-to-eat prunes
juice of 1 lemon
15ml/1 tbsp clear honey
1.5ml/¼ tsp saffron strands
1 cinnamon stick, broken in half
50g/2oz/½ cup flaked (sliced) almonds, toasted
salt and ground black pepper

For the couscous

450g/1lb/2½ cups couscous
25g/1oz/2 tbsp butter
30ml/2 tbsp chopped fresh coriander (cilantro)

1 Trim the lamb and cut it into 2.5cm/1in cubes. Heat the butter and oil in a large flameproof tagine or casserole until foaming. Add the onion, garlic and ginger, and cook, stirring occasionally, until the onion has softened but not coloured.

2 Add the lamb pieces and red pepper, and mix well. Pour in the lamb stock or water.

3 Add the prunes, lemon juice, honey, saffron strands and cinnamon. Season with salt and pepper, and stir well.

4 Bring to the boil, then reduce the heat and cover the tagine or casserole with a lid. Simmer for 1½–2 hours, stirring occasionally, until the meat is melt-in-the-mouth tender.

5 Place the couscous in a bowl and cover with salted water, stirring. Set aside for 10 minutes. Stir in the butter, and chopped fresh coriander.

6 Pile the couscous into a large, warmed serving dish or on to individual warmed bowls or plates.

7 Taste the stew for seasoning, and add more salt and pepper to taste, if necessary. Ladle the stew on to the couscous and scatter the toasted flaked almonds over the top.

Energy 652kcal/2716kJ; Protein 35.2g; Carbohydrate 30.9g, of which sugars 26g; Fat 44.2g, of which saturates 16.4g; Cholesterol 141mg; Calcium 97mg; Fibre 5.4g; Sodium 223mg.

Beef tagine with sweet potatoes

Fes is credited with Morocco's finest tagines. This is a particularly good one, the sweet potatoes and warm spices providing a mellow contrast to the robust flavour of the beef. If you do not have a tagine, use a casserole with a tight-fitting lid to create the effect of cooking in the traditional Moroccan pot.

SERVES FOUR

- 675–900g/1½–2lb braising or stewing beef
- 30ml/2 tbsp sunflower oil
- a good pinch of ground turmeric
- 1 large onion, chopped
- 1 fresh red or green chilli, seeded and finely chopped
- 7.5ml/1½ tsp paprika
- a good pinch of cayenne pepper
- 2.5ml/½ tsp ground cumin
- 450g/1lb sweet potatoes
- 15ml/1 tbsp chopped fresh flat leaf parsley
- 15ml/1 tbsp chopped fresh coriander (cilantro)
- 15g/½oz/1 tbsp butter
- salt and ground black pepper

VARIATIONS

- You can use lean lamb instead of beef, for a different taste.
- Try sliced swede (rutabaga) in place of the sweet potatoes, for an earthy variation.

1 Trim the meat of excess fat, and cut it into 2cm/¾in cubes. Heat the oil in a flameproof tagine or casserole, and fry the meat, with the turmeric and seasoning, over a medium heat for 3–4 minutes, until the meat is evenly browned, stirring frequently.

2 Cover the pan tightly with a lid and cook for 15 minutes over a fairly gentle heat, without lifting the lid. Preheat the oven to 180°C/350°F/Gas 4.

3 Add the onion, chilli, paprika, cayenne pepper and cumin to the pan together with just enough water to cover the meat. Cover tightly and cook in the oven for 1–1½ hours, until the meat is very tender, checking occasionally and adding a little extra water, if necessary, to keep the stew fairly moist.

4 Meanwhile, peel the sweet potatoes and slice them straight into a bowl of salted water to avoid discolouring. Transfer to a pan, bring to the boil, then simmer for 2–3 minutes. Drain.

5 Stir most of the herbs into the meat, adding a little extra water if it appears dry. Arrange the potato slices over the meat and dot with the butter. Cover and cook in the oven for 10 minutes more, until the potatoes are tender.

6 Increase the oven temperature to 200°C/400°F/Gas 6 or preheat the grill (broiler) to its hottest setting.

7 Remove the lid and cook in the oven or under the grill for 5–10 minutes, until the sweet potatoes are golden. Serve, garnished with the rest of the herbs.

Energy 434Kcal/1819kJ; Protein 39.1g; Carbohydrate 28.9g, of which sugars 10g; Fat 18.8g, of which saturates 6.8g; Cholesterol 114mg; Calcium 66mg; Fibre 3.9g; Sodium 180mg.

Tagine of beef with peas and saffron

This tagine is a popular supper dish, and can be made with beef or lamb. Saffron imparts a distinctive taste and delicate colour. The peas, tomatoes and tangy lemon added towards the end of the cooking time enliven the rich, gingery beef mixture, and the brown olives finish it off.

SERVES 6

1.2kg/2½lb braising or stewing steak
30ml/2 tbsp olive oil
1 onion, chopped
25g/1oz fresh root ginger, peeled and chopped
5ml/1 tsp ground ginger
a pinch of cayenne pepper
a pinch of saffron threads
2 tomatoes
1.2kg/2½lb shelled fresh peas
1 preserved lemon, chopped
a handful of brown kalamata olives
salt and ground black pepper
crusty bread, to serve

1 Trim the meat of excess fat, and cut it into 2cm/¾in cubes.

2 Place the steak into a flameproof tagine or casserole with the olive oil, chopped onion, fresh and ground ginger, cayenne pepper and saffron, and season with salt and pepper.

3 Pour in enough water to cover the meat completely and bring to the boil. Then reduce the heat, cover with a lid, and simmer for about 1½ hours, or until the meat is very tender. Cook for a little longer, if necessary.

4 Meanwhile, to peel the tomatoes, score a cross through the skin and place in boiling water for 30 seconds. Peel away the skins, and chop the flesh.

5 When the meat is very tender, add the peas, tomatoes, preserved lemon and olives. Stir well and cook, uncovered, for about 10 minutes, or until the peas are tender and the sauce has reduced.

6 Taste to check the seasoning, and add salt and pepper if necessary. Serve the tagine with crusty bread.

Energy 492Kcal/2049kJ; Protein 57.9g; Carbohydrate 25.6g, of which sugars 7g; Fat 18.2g, of which saturates 6g; Cholesterol 126mg; Calcium 61mg; Fibre 10.1g; Sodium 134mg.

Beef tfaia tagine with cinnamon couscous

Regarded as a grand tagine, beef tfaia is usually on the menu of restaurants in Fes, Marrakesh and Meknes. Traditionally a 'tfaia' dish should include softened onions and sultanas flavoured with saffron and other spices. This mixture can be cooked as part of the dish, or served separately on top of the beef.

SERVES 4

500g/1lb 2oz lean beef
1 onion, finely chopped
2–3 garlic cloves, finely chopped
5ml/1 tsp ground coriander
5ml/1 tsp ground cumin
4–6 cardamom pods
a fingerful of saffron fronds
salt and ground black pepper

For the couscous

350g/12oz couscous
2.5ml/½ tsp sea salt
400ml/14fl oz warm water
15–30ml/1–2 tbsp sunflower oil
15g/½oz butter
5–10ml/1–2 tsp ground cinnamon

For the tfaia

15ml/1 tbsp olive oil
15ml/1 tbsp butter
2–3 onions, thinly sliced
30ml/2 tbsp sultanas (golden raisins)
2–3 cinnamon sticks
5ml/1 tsp saffron fronds, soaked in 2–3 tbsp warm water
30ml/2 tbsp honey
salt and ground black pepper

1 Preheat the oven to 180°C/350°F/Gas 4. Slice the meat into strips. Place it in a flameproof tagine or casserole with the onion, garlic and spices.

2 Pour in just enough water to cover the meat. Bring it to the boil, then reduce the heat, cover with the lid, and simmer for 40 minutes, or until very tender.

3 Place the couscous in an ovenproof dish. Stir the salt into the water, and pour it over the couscous. Cover, then leave the couscous to absorb the water for 10–15 minutes.

4 Using your fingers, rub the oil into the couscous to separate the grains, lifting them into the air to aerate them. Sprinkle the butter over the top. Place a piece of dampened baking parchment over the top of the couscous and cook in the oven for 15–20 minutes to heat through.

5 Meanwhile, for the tfaia, heat the oil with the butter in a heavy pan, and add the onions. Cook for 3–4 minutes, stirring, until the onions begin to soften.

6 Add the sultanas, cinnamon sticks, saffron and soaking water, honey and seasoning. Reduce the heat, cover with a lid, and cook gently for 15 minutes.

7 Transfer the couscous to a serving dish, piling it in a mound. Create a well in the top and dust the couscous with cinnamon, or sprinkle it in lines down the side of the couscous like the spokes of a wheel.

8 Using a slotted spoon, lift the beef into the couscous well and arrange the tfaia over it. Season the beef cooking liquid with salt and pepper, and strain it into a small bowl to serve with the dish.

VARIATION

You can make the same recipe with lamb instead of beef, or you can omit the meat and make a plain couscous 'tfaia' which can be served with almost any meat or poultry tagine.

Energy 554kcal/2316kJ; Protein 35.3g;Carbohydrate 67.7g, of which sugars 19.4g; Fat 17.5g, of which saturates 6.3g; Cholesterol 86mg; Calcium 98mg; Fibre 3g; Sodium 126mg.

Vegetables

Fresh vegetables are abundant in Morocco, and market traders sell a variety of produce from the local farms, as well as imported crops. Mediterranean staples, such as aubergines (eggplants), courgettes (zucchini), tomatoes and artichokes are put to good use alongside hearty root vegetables such as potatoes, carrots and yams. Beans add protein and texture to vegetable-rich tagines, and a medley of spices and seasonings turn simple ingredients into show-stopping dishes.

Baked vegetable tagine with harissa yogurt

This village tagine from the middle Atlas region of Morocco can be served as a side dish, or on its own with yogurt and chunks of crusty bread. Traditionally this dish is baked in a communal oven, but at home you can use a heavy shallow casserole, or an earthenware baking dish.

SERVES 4–6

30–45ml/2–3 tbsp olive or argan oil
2 onions, halved and sliced with the grain
4 garlic cloves, chopped
1–2 red chillies, seeded and chopped
10ml/2 tsp cumin seeds
10ml/2 tsp coriander seeds
10ml/2 tsp ground turmeric
6 potatoes, peeled and thickly sliced
2–3 carrots, peeled and thickly sliced
1 head of green, leafy cabbage, trimmed and thickly sliced
about 900ml/1½ pints/3¾ cups vegetable stock
225g/8oz fresh or frozen peas (defrosted, if frozen)
a bunch of fresh flat leaf parsley, finely chopped
a bunch of fresh mint, finely chopped
4–6 large tomatoes, sliced
15g/½oz/1 tbsp butter, cut into small pieces
salt and ground black pepper
crusty bread, to serve

For the yogurt

500g/1¼lb/2 cups thick, creamy yogurt
2 garlic cloves, crushed
5–10ml/1–2 tsp harissa paste
salt and ground black pepper

VARIATION

You can alter the vegetable selection with whatever is in season, such as broccoli, pumpkin, artichokes, sweet potato or courgettes (zucchini).

1 Preheat the oven to 180°C/350°F/Gas 4. Heat the oil in a flameproof tagine or casserole. Add the onions and cook, stirring, for 2–3 minutes, until they begin to colour. Add the garlic, chillies, cumin seeds and coriander seeds, and cook, stirring, for 1–2 minutes.

2 Stir in the turmeric, potatoes, carrots and cabbage, then pour in the stock and mix the vegetables thoroughly with the spices and onions.

3 Put the lid on the tagine, or cover the dish with foil, and place it in the oven for about 25 minutes, or until the potatoes and carrots are tender but still retain a little bite.

4 Add the peas and most of the fresh parsley and mint, reserving a little for the garnish. Season with salt and pepper.

5 Arrange the tomato slices, overlapping each other, on top of the vegetables and sprinkle the pieces of butter over the top.

6 Place the tagine back into the oven, uncovered, for 15–20 minutes, until the tomatoes are lightly browned on top.

7 Meanwhile, beat the yogurt in a bowl with the garlic. Stir in the harissa, and season to taste with salt and pepper. Set aside until the tagine is ready.

8 Garnish the tagine with the rest of the parsley and mint, and serve with spoonfuls of the harissa yogurt and chunks of crusty bread.

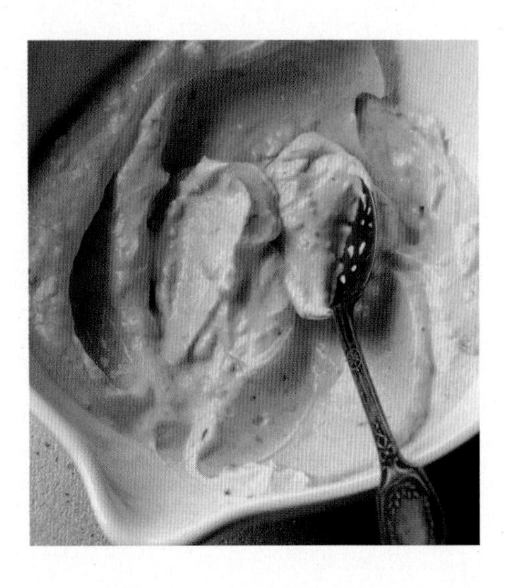

Energy 284kcal/1188kJ; Protein 13.9g; Carbohydrate 32.4g, of which sugars 21.9g; Fat 13.9g, of which saturates 4.7g; Cholesterol 29mg; Calcium 362mg; Fibre 9.5g; Sodium 134mg.

Mixed bean and aubergine tagine with mint yogurt

In this traditional-style Moroccan dish, the mixed beans and aubergine provide both texture and taste, which are enhanced by flavourful herbs and chillies. A mixture of courgettes (zucchini) and red and yellow (bell) peppers can be used instead of the aubergine, if you like.

SERVES 4

- 115g/4oz/generous ½ cup dried red kidney beans, soaked overnight in cold water and drained
- 115g/4oz/generous ½ cup dried black-eyed beans (peas) or cannellini beans, soaked overnight in cold water and drained
- 2 bay leaves
- 2 celery sticks, each cut into 4 batons
- 75ml/5 tbsp olive oil
- 1 aubergine (eggplant), about 350g/12oz, cut into chunks
- 1 onion, thinly sliced
- 3 garlic cloves, crushed
- 1–2 fresh red chillies, seeded and finely chopped
- 30ml/2 tbsp tomato purée (paste)
- 5ml/1 tsp paprika
- 2 large tomatoes, roughly chopped
- 300ml/½ pint/1¼ cups vegetable stock
- 15ml/1 tbsp each chopped fresh coriander (cilantro), mint and parsley
- salt and ground black pepper
- a few fresh coriander leaves, to garnish

For the mint yogurt

- 150g/5oz/⅔ cup natural (plain) yogurt
- 30ml/2 tbsp chopped fresh mint
- 2 spring onions (scallions), chopped

COOK'S TIP

Dried red kidney beans need to be soaked overnight and cooked well, as they contain toxins when raw.

1 Place the soaked and drained kidney beans in a large pan of unsalted boiling water. Bring back to the boil and boil rapidly for 10 minutes, then drain. Place the soaked and drained black-eyed or cannellini beans in a separate large pan of boiling unsalted water and boil rapidly for 10 minutes, then drain.

2 Place 600ml/1 pint/2½ cups of water in a large tagine or casserole, and add the bay leaves, celery and beans. Cover and place in an unheated oven. Set the oven to 190°C/375°F/Gas 5. Cook for 1–1½ hours or until the beans are tender. Drain and set aside.

3 Heat 60ml/4 tbsp of the oil in a frying pan or flameproof tagine. Add the aubergine and cook, stirring, for 4–5 minutes, until browned. Remove from the pan and set aside.

4 Add the remaining oil to the frying pan or tagine, then add the onion. Cook, stirring, for 4–5 minutes, until softened.

5 Add the garlic and chillies, and cook for a further 5 minutes, stirring frequently, until the onion is golden.

6 Reduce the oven temperature to 160°C/325°F/Gas 3. Add the tomato purée and paprika and cook, stirring, for 1–2 minutes. Add the tomatoes, browned aubergine, drained beans and stock. Season with salt and pepper.

7 Cover the tagine with the lid or, if using a frying pan, transfer the contents to a clay tagine or casserole. Place in the oven and cook for 1 hour.

8 Meanwhile, mix together the yogurt, mint and spring onions, and place in a small serving dish.

9 To serve, add the fresh coriander, mint and parsley to the tagine and lightly mix through the vegetables. Season to taste with salt and pepper. Garnish with some fresh coriander leaves, and serve with the mint yogurt.

Energy 328Kcal/1377kJ; Protein 14.9g; Carbohydrate 35.2g, of which sugars 9.3g; Fat 15.3g, of which saturates 2.2g; Cholesterol 0mg; Calcium 96mg; Fibre 12.8g; Sodium 28mg.

Tagine of artichoke hearts, potatoes, peas and saffron

When artichokes are in season, this succulent tagine is one of my favourite country dishes made using other produce from the garden or fields as well. Fresh coriander, parsley and mint combine to complement the summery flavours of the vegetables, while turmeric contributes its earthy warmth.

SERVES 4–6

6 fresh artichoke hearts
juice of 1 lemon
30–45ml/2–3 tbsp olive oil
1 onion, chopped
675g/1½lb potatoes, peeled and quartered
a small bunch of fresh coriander (cilantro), chopped
a small bunch of fresh mint, chopped
a small bunch of fresh flat leaf parsley, chopped
a pinch of saffron threads
5ml/1 tsp ground turmeric
about 350ml/12fl oz/1½ cups vegetable stock
finely chopped rind of ½ preserved lemon
250g/9oz/2¼ cups peas
salt and ground black pepper
bread, to serve

COOK'S TIPS

- Prepare the artichokes yourself by removing the outer leaves, cutting off the stems, and scooping out the choke and hairy fibres with a teaspoon. Alternatively, buy frozen prepared artichoke hearts.
- Once cut, the flesh of artichokes will blacken. To prevent this from happening, put the artichokes into acidulated water – you can use lemon juice or white wine vinegar.

1 Poach the artichoke hearts very gently in plenty of simmering water with half the lemon juice, for 10–15 minutes until tender. Drain and refresh under cold running water, then drain again. Set aside.

2 Heat the olive oil in a flameproof tagine or heavy pan. Add the chopped onion and cook over a low heat for about 15 minutes, or until softened but not browned.

3 Add the potatoes, along with the fresh coriander and mint, most of the parsley, the remaining lemon juice, and the saffron and turmeric to the pan.

4 Pour in the vegetable stock and bring to the boil, then reduce the heat, cover the pan and simmer for about 15 minutes, or until the potatoes are almost tender.

5 Add the finely chopped preserved lemon, artichoke hearts and peas to the stew, then stir to combine. Cook the tagine, uncovered, for a further 10 minutes.

6 Taste to check the seasoning, adding salt and pepper to taste if necessary. Sprinkle with the remaining parsley, and serve with chunks of fresh bread.

Energy 260Kcal/1089kJ; Protein 8.6g; Carbohydrate 42g, of which sugars 10.6g; Fat 7.5g, of which saturates 1.2g; Cholesterol 0mg; Calcium 96mg; Fibre 7.9g; Sodium 47mg.

Tagine of yam, carrots and prunes

The vegetables in this succulent, syrupy tagine should be slightly caramelized. They are at their best served with grilled meats, couscous or with lots of warm, crusty bread and a leafy, herb-filled salad. I first had this dish in a tiny hut in the Atlas Mountains. The air was cold and the food was warming – it was quite delicious. You can make this either with yam (also known as taro) or sweet potato.

SERVES 4–6

25–30 pickling (pearl) or button onions
45ml/3 tbsp olive oil
a little butter
900g/2lb yam (taro) or sweet potato, peeled and cut into bitesize chunks
2–3 carrots, cut into bitesize chunks
150g/5oz/generous ½ cup ready-to-eat pitted prunes
5ml/1 tsp ground cinnamon
2.5ml/½ tsp ground ginger
10ml/2 tsp clear honey
450ml/¾ pint/scant 2 cups vegetable stock
a small bunch of fresh coriander (cilantro), finely chopped
a small bunch of fresh mint, finely chopped
salt and ground black pepper

1 Preheat the oven to 200°C/400°F/Gas 6. First, blanch the pickling or button onions in boiling water for 1 minute, then refresh immediately under cold water. Peel the onions – the skin should come away easily.

2 Heat the olive oil in a flameproof tagine or casserole with the butter, and stir in the peeled onions. Cook for about 5 minutes until the onions are tender. Remove half of the onions from the pan, and set them aside.

3 Add the chunks of yam or sweet potato and carrots to the onions remaining in the pan, and cook until lightly browned.

4 Stir in the prunes with the cinnamon, ginger and honey, then pour in the stock. Season well with salt and pepper, then cover the tagine or casserole with a lid, and transfer to the oven. Cook for 45 minutes.

5 Add the reserved onions, put the lid back on, and bake for a further 10 minutes.

6 Gently stir in the chopped fresh coriander and mint, and serve the tagine immediately.

COOK'S TIP

The yam or taro has brown skin and cream-coloured flesh; the sweet potato has dark red or orange skin and orange flesh. When buying yams and sweet potatoes, buy firm specimens that do not 'give' when pressed.

Energy 454Kcal/1922kJ; Protein 6.2g; Carbohydrate 91.8g, of which sugars 27.1g; Fat 9.5g, of which saturates 1.5g; Cholesterol 0mg; Calcium 111mg; Fibre 7.9g; Sodium 32mg.

Tagine of butter beans, cherry tomatoes and olives

Serve this hearty butter bean dish with grills or roasts, particularly fish. It is substantial enough to be served on its own, with a leafy salad and fresh, crusty bread. In and around Tangier, where the Spanish influence remains quite strong, bean dishes like this often include a spicy sausage like chorizo. This would be added with the onion to lend its flavour to the whole dish, if you are not serving to vegetarians.

SERVES 4

115g/4oz/⅔ cup butter (lima) beans, soaked overnight
30–45ml/2–3 tbsp olive oil
1 onion, chopped
2–3 garlic cloves, crushed
25g/1oz fresh root ginger, peeled and chopped
a pinch of saffron threads
16 cherry tomatoes
a generous pinch of sugar
a handful of fleshy black olives, pitted
5ml/1 tsp ground cinnamon
5ml/1 tsp paprika
a small bunch of fresh flat leaf parsley
salt and ground black pepper

1 Rinse the soaked butter beans and place them in a large pan with plenty of water. Bring to the boil, and boil for 10 minutes, then reduce the heat and simmer gently for 1–1½ hours, until tender.

2 Drain the beans and refresh under cold water. Set aside.

3 Heat the olive oil in a flameproof tagine or heavy pan. Add the onion, garlic and ginger, and cook for about 10 minutes, or until softened but not browned.

4 Stir in the saffron threads, followed by the cherry tomatoes and sugar.

5 As the tomatoes begin to soften, stir in the butter beans. When the tomatoes have heated through, stir in the olives, ground cinnamon and paprika.

6 Season to taste with salt and pepper, then sprinkle over the parsley leaves. Discard the stalks. Serve immediately.

COOK'S TIP

If you are in a hurry, you could use two 400g/14oz cans of butter beans for this tagine. Make sure you rinse the beans well before adding to the tagine as canned beans tend to be salty.

Energy 146Kcal/615kJ; Protein 7.4g; Carbohydrate 16.2g, of which sugars 3.8g; Fat 6.3g, of which saturates 0.9g; Cholesterol 0mg; Calcium 62mg; Fibre 6g; Sodium 16mg.

Okra and tomato tagine

This vegetable stew is a North African speciality, and is especially common in Morocco. Okra is also known as 'ladies' fingers'; a reference to their tapered shape. When cut before being cooked, as in this recipe, the pods ooze a glue-like substance which gives the dish a distinctive texture.

SERVES 4
350g/12oz okra
5–6 tomatoes
2 small onions
2 garlic cloves, crushed
1 fresh green chilli, seeded
5ml/1 tsp paprika
a small handful of fresh coriander (cilantro)
30ml/2 tbsp sunflower oil
juice of 1 lemon

1 Trim the okra and then cut them into 1cm/½in lengths.

2 To peel the tomatoes, score a cross through the skins, then place them in boiling water for 30 seconds, and remove with a slotted spoon. Once cool enough to handle, peel the skin away – it should come away easily. Cut the tomatoes into quarters, and remove and discard the seeds. Roughly chop the flesh.

3 Roughly chop one of the onions and place it in a blender or food processor with the garlic, chilli, paprika, coriander and 60ml/4 tbsp water. Process to make a paste.

4 Thinly slice the second onion. Heat the sunflower oil in a flameproof tagine or heavy pan, add the sliced onion, and fry it for 5–6 minutes, until golden brown. Transfer the onion to a plate and set it aside.

VARIATIONS
- Use 3–4 shallots instead of the onions, if you like.
- For a spicier tagine, leave the seeds in the chilli.

5 Reduce the heat, and place the onion and coriander paste into the tagine or pan. Cook the paste over a medium heat for 1–2 minutes, stirring frequently.

6 Add the okra, tomatoes, lemon juice and about 120ml/4fl oz/½ cup water. Stir well to mix, then cover tightly with a lid, and simmer over a low heat for about 15 minutes, or until the okra is tender.

7 Transfer the okra and tomato tagine to a serving dish, if you like, sprinkle with the fried onion slices, and serve immediately.

Energy 115Kcal/482kJ; Protein 4.2g; Carbohydrate 9.6g, of which sugars 8.5g; Fat 7g, of which saturates 1.2g; Cholesterol 0mg; Calcium 182mg; Fibre 6g; Sodium 26mg.

Chickpea tagine

The preserved lemon in this recipe shows you that it comes from Morocco, where the distinctive yellow globes in glass jars glimmer like miniature suns in the markets. The flavour of preserved – or pickled – lemon is wonderful. Slightly salty, less tart than the fresh fruit, it adds a real zing to chickpeas.

SERVES 4

- 150g/5oz/¾ cup chickpeas, soaked overnight, or 2 x 400g/14oz cans chickpeas, rinsed and drained
- 30ml/2 tbsp sunflower oil
- 1 large onion, chopped
- 1 garlic clove, crushed (optional)
- 400g/14oz can chopped tomatoes
- 5ml/1 tsp ground cumin
- 350ml/12fl oz/1½ cups vegetable stock
- ¼ preserved lemon
- 30ml/2 tbsp chopped fresh coriander (cilantro)
- bread, to serve

1 If using dried chickpeas, cook the soaked chickpeas in plenty of boiling water for 1–1½ hours, until tender. Drain well. Place the chickpeas in a bowl of cold water and rub them between your fingers to remove the skins.

2 Heat the oil in a flameproof tagine or casserole, add the onion and garlic, if using, and fry for 8–10 minutes, stirring often, until golden.

3 Add the chickpeas, tomatoes, cumin and stock, and stir well to combine. Bring to the boil, then reduce the heat and simmer, uncovered, for 30–40 minutes, until the chickpeas are very soft and most of the liquid has evaporated.

4 Rinse the preserved lemon under cold running water, and cut away the flesh and pith.

5 Cut the peel into thin slivers, and stir it into the chickpea mixture together with most of the chopped fresh coriander.

6 Garnish with the rest of the fresh coriander, and serve immediately with chunks of crusty Moroccan bread.

Energy 207Kcal/871kJ; Protein 9.7g; Carbohydrate 26.4g, of which sugars 7.1g; Fat 7.8g, of which saturates 0.9g; Cholesterol 0mg; Calcium 87mg; Fibre 5.6g; Sodium 56mg.

Index